Quail Keeping for Money:
Read this Book Before Starting Your Quail Keeping Career

Table Of Content

Introduction

I would like to thank and congratulate you on downloading *"Quail Keeping for Money: Read this Book Before Starting Your Quail Keeping Career!"* If you learn the best way to go about running your own quail farming operation, you can do very well at this. Of course, one of the most important steps in being successful at it is to make sure that you start off with a nice healthy flock of quails. Learning the steps, you need to take to raise a healthy flock of quails will be vital in helping to ensure that you will profit from this career choice.

Like for most businesses, it is always a clever idea to have a business plan, this also applies with the successful running of a quail farm. You will need to come up with a business plan and stick with it religiously. In general, it is a clever idea to have a business plan for any business venture. Getting a business plan setup for the running of your quail farm is going to help to guide you in the direction of making a profit from it. The first chapter of this book covers have a good quail farming business plan in place.

Chapter 1. Having a Quail Farming Business Plan in Place

You will need to stick to your business plan, for you to breath life into it. Creating a good solid business plan is a clever idea before you start your business venture. When you have your business plan in order it is going to help lead you towards being successful with a result that involves making a profit from your quail farming business.

When first starting into the quail farming business, it is a clever idea to visit local quail farms in your area, talk to others who are in this business, ask them how they raise quails successfully. Even if you must pay them a small fee to gain this information, it could be well worth the investment. You want to gain valuable information that can help you to learn the best way you can raise your quail flock to be strong and healthy. It would be worth your effort to visit successful local quail farmers and seek their advice and tips on how you can raise your quail flock to be healthy and good producers of eggs.

When you write up your quail farming business plan, you should make sure that you are very clear on the goal that you are trying to reach. Ask yourself some questions such as the following:

What is the purpose behind you raising quails?

Ask yourself what is your reason for wanting to raise quails—is it just for personal reasons or for commercial reasons? Do you just want to provide yourself and loved ones with fresh eggs or are you looking to build a business from raising quails?

What are the products you can produce from quails?

Before you decide what products, you want to focus on producing, you need to do some research and find out what bird products are popular right now. This is very valuable information for you to know when you finally begin your quail farming.

There are four areas that you can choose from:

- Breeding—selling fertilized eggs, day old quail chicks, or a week or two old etc.
- Raising for egg production
- Raising for meat production
- Raising quails for meat and egg production

Housing your quails:

To keep your quails safe and secure, you will need to supply them with the necessary requirements. If your quails are in an environment where they feel safe and secure this will help them to be more productive. You can raise quails on floors or cages. You want to ensure that the housing you choose for your quails is properly ventilated, and they always have a fresh supply of water, and well-balanced feeds.

Hire Laborer for quail farm:

If you are planning to run a large size quail farm you should take into consideration hiring a laborer to help you with the running of your quail farm. Looking after quails requires very minimal help, they are easy to manage. Of course, you can enlist your own loved ones to help pitch in with the caring of your quails.

Quality quail feeds:

The level of quality of products that you will produce from your quail farm will largely depend upon the quality of feeds you are feeding your quails. Quails are known to be fussy eaters, make sure that you provide them with well-balanced feeds, placing them in an area where they have easy access to them.

A healthy adult quail can on average consume 30grams of feed per day. Make sure that the feeds you choose for your quails contain a good amount of proteins in them. Your quails will need protein to produce healthy eggs and maintain healthy feathers.

You can feed your quails turkey or chicken feed. They will consume less feeds compared to other poultry birds such as turkeys and chickens. When it comes time for you to invest your capital, it will be less than if you were raising other poultry birds such as chickens.

Breeding quails:

An adult male quail can easily take care of five females a day, for breeding. It is a good idea to have one male for every three females. Quail females are not very good egg hatchers since becoming domesticated. Invest in a good egg incubator to help you to hatch the eggs. That is only necessary if you plan to keep your quails for breeding purposes.

Quail care:

There are several diseases that effect other poultry birds, but quails are resistant to their effects. Quails are prone to getting infections due to improper care and poor management of them. If you make the effort to take proper care of your quails, you will be protecting them against health-related issues. This will help to ensure that you will benefit for your efforts through profit from your quail farming.

Marketing quail products:

Create a good marketing strategy to help ensure that you will gain profit from your quail farming. If you have a good market strategy in place this will help to enable you to sell your quail products at good competitive prices.

Figure out what your total costs will be for producing your quail products, then you can make your total selling cost higher than what your total cost of production was, leaving you with a profit.

There are various ways that you can sell your quail eggs, you might choose to go to the local farmer's market in your area, or you can supply them in crates to your local grocery store, or even sell them on the internet. You may also decide to package and sell your quail meat to local stores.

Chapter 2. Everything You Need to Know About Quail Eggs

The female quail will begin to lay eggs at only six weeks old. The female quail can lay on average about 25 eggs in a month, which is 300 eggs a year. The Japanese quails are well-known for producing these kinds of numbers with egg laying. Now you are beginning to understand and learn what you are going to have in store for you when it comes to getting into running your own quail farm. Now let us look further into the details of running a quail farm.

There are several approaches you can take to starting into the quail farming business. The most common two ways are either by starting with hatching quail eggs that are fertile into chicks through incubating the eggs, or going with live birds (preferably quail chicks) from local breeders or quail farmers. It is very important that you learn how to identify good quail eggs that will be suitable for incubation.

Learning to identify unsuitable quail eggs for incubation:

This is a crucial part of the incubation process that you know how to tell if eggs are fertile and suitable for incubation. Possessing these skills will help you to avoid incubating abnormal and unfertilized eggs which in turn could lead to you suffering massive losses of resources and time. You want to be operating your quail farm at a profit not a loss. This is a step that will help to ensure this.

It will be somewhat of a challenge to learn how to tell the difference between a normal and abnormal quail egg. It would be a very disappointing process for you to find that the quail eggs you thought were healthy fertilized eggs ended up being abnormal or infertile.

This could be a very costly mistake in time and money. The list below points out what to look for in eggs that are unsuitable for incubation.

- Very thin eggshells
- Cracks on the eggshell
- Double yolk
- Bloody spots on the yolk of the egg, this you can detect by candling.

Verify fertility of incubated quail eggs:

The first step you need to take to help to ensure you will have fertilized eggs is to make a good pairing of your quails: one male to a maximum of three female quails. On the seventh day of incubation you can candle the eggs to check to see if they are fertile. When you candle you will be able to see either a clear embryo which is an infertile egg, or a reddish embryo which is a fertile egg.

If you are unsure about the colors try again on candling about the 14th day of incubation. If the chick is present in the egg the egg is going to look darker. If the chick is absent the larger part of the will be clear. Make sure to be careful when you are doing the candling process so that you do not damage the eggs.

Incubation

Get yourself a good incubator for your quail eggs. The incubator should offer a suitable temperature that is relative to humidity and offer adequate supply of fresh air. You need to turn your quail eggs 180^0 three times within a 24-hour period. This step will help to ensure that your quail eggs are heated evenly, except for the last three days of hatching, or day 15 onwards.

Incubating your quail eggs successfully:

It will take between 18 to 24 days for your quail eggs to hatch. There are mutants of quails that their eggs take an average of 14 to 17 days to hatch. You can take proper steps to help ensure that the rate of your eggs hatching is high. Eggs that have been incubated for 7 days or less have a higher chance of hatching. Eggs that are older than ten days have a lower rate of hatching.

To help ensure that you will increase your hatch rate only use eggs that are several days or less in your incubation process. Make sure that you keep your incubator disinfected and clean. The temperatures within your incubator should range from 99.5^0 to 100^0 Fahrenheit. Read the instructions of your incubator to make sure that you handle the best you can according to the instructions from the manufacturer of it.

Place your eggs at room temperature a few hours before you place the inside the incubator. Make sure that the eggs are nice and clean, and free from any abnormalities, candle check your quail eggs. You must keep your incubator at a suitable temperature to get the result of hatched quail eggs. Have fresh air, and relative humidity.

If your incubator is a manual one, it is important that you remember to turn the eggs three times within a 24-hour period and to make sure that the heat is evenly dispersed over your eggs. Next, we will consider poor egg-hatch and the solutions for each cause. Below you will find six of the leading causes of poor egg-hatch and the solutions for them:

Incubating infertile eggs:

It can be very frustrating not to mention disappointing to discover that your quail eggs you were incubating turned out to be infertile.

Solution: Candle your eggs before and during the incubation process (before the 15th day) to help you to detect any infertile eggs. Make sure that you have properly paired your quails, one male to three females. This is going to help to ensure that the eggs will indeed be fertilized.

Incubating defective/abnormal eggs:

Quail eggs are abnormal or defective if they have cracks in the shell, double yolk, absence of yolk, bloody spots all of these factors are found in defective or abnormal eggs.

Solution:

It is important that you candle your eggs before you incubate them, so that the abnormal eggs are not taking up valuable space within your incubator. Collect your quail eggs at least two times a day, store the eggs in a humid room with pointy end facing upwards.

Failure to turn incubated eggs:

Turning your quail eggs will help to ensure that they are evenly warmed. If you do not do this you could run the risk of overheating an area of the egg which will make it unsuitable for hatching chicks.

Solution:

Make sure during the incubating process that you are turning the eggs at least three times in every twenty-four-hour period. If you use an automatic incubator it can turn the eggs 180° angle three times a day.

If conditions of incubator are unfavorable:

Make sure that there is the proper amount of fresh air and temperatures, as well as relative humidity so that your quail eggs can hatch successfully.

Solution:

Choose an incubator that can hatch eggs. Keep the incubator clean and disinfected. If you are in an area that tends to have a lot of power failures, it would be well worth your while to have power backup.

Eggs looked fertile but did not hatch:

This could happen to you if you are incubating eggs that are from older quail breeds. It could also occur due to you waiting too long after the eggs were laid to place them into the incubator.

Solution:

Incubate eggs from young quail pairs. Choose the eggs that are seven days old or less. Do not hold eggs in your holding facility for more than eight days, as this can lessen the chances of the eggs hatching. Do not wash any eggs that are dirty, this can cause the natural protective layer of the egg to be washed off, exposing entry by organisms, hampering the ability of you being able to hatch your quail eggs successfully.

Not managing your quail egg incubator well: If you are not managing the temperatures and humidity of your incubator properly, this could result in your quail eggs not hatching. If your incubator is dirty this too can result in poor hatching results.

Solution:

Make sure you have the proper temperatures and humidity during incubation process. Keep your incubator in a room that the temperature does not fluctuate and will allow humidity to occur. Make sure that you disinfect and clean your incubator before using it.

Chapter 3. Caring for Your Quail Chicks

It will take your quail chicks between 18 to 24 days to hatch on average, when it has been successfully incubated. When the chicks finally do hatch, you may notice that they have an egg yolk attachment on their abdomen. Do not remove it as they will use this as a source of food for the next few days. This will allow them to have time to adjust to their new surroundings, and their new life outside of the egg. Do not worry that the chicks are tiny, they will have the ability to feed themselves. Remember that they are sensitive to cold and hot temperatures. To avoid your quail chicks from drowning in water troughs fill them half-way with small marbles.

There are two ways that you can go about getting quail chicks. You can choose to get them from a local quail breeder or go through the incubation process and successfully incubate your own eggs. After the chicks have hatched you will need to transfer them to a brooder. Below are some tips on what a good quail chick brooder should consist of:

Source of heat:

To keep the temperatures regulated within your brooder you will need a good source of heat. You can choose to use heat sources such as heat lamps, charcoal burners, or gas burners. The brooder needs to be heated properly.

The two best ways for you to ensure this is to use a thermometer or keep close observation on the behavior of your quail chicks and what they are doing around the heat source. If you notice that the chicks are crowding around the brooder, this is a clear sign that there is a cold source in the brooder somewhere. If on the other hand the chicks are staying far away from the heat source this is a sign that the heat is too high.

Once you have reached a nice temperature within your quail chick brooder the chicks should be evenly dispersed around the brooder. You should try to maintain a temperature of 95^0 Fahrenheit during the first week.

After the first week, it should be lowered by five degrees on each passing week until they are ready to be taken out of the brooder. You should be able to remove the source of heat from brooder after the fourth week. Allow your quails to adapt to their surroundings.

Litter:

You can help to keep your brooder warm by using litter, it will help to absorb moisture. You can get litter in the form of wood shavings or sawdust. The litter that has been used must be discarded from the brooder to avoid spillage of any undesired odor from the brooder to adjacent surroundings.

Feeders:

Place nice and clean feeders at convenient spots where your quail chicks are not straining to access them. The feeders need to be designed in such a way so as to prevent the chicks from defecating in them. Make sure that you supply your quail chicks with well-balanced quality feeds. You can feed your quails on game bird feed or turkey feeds as a starter feed that will offer and average of about 25% protein.

When your quails are four weeks old you should change their feed to layers' mash. Since your quail chicks will begin laying eggs at six weeks, it is a clever idea to change to mash as your quails begin to reach egg laying stage in their development.

Correct amount of light

You want to make sure that your brooder has the correct amount of light, so your chicks can see the feed and water sources. You can use a bulb as a light source in a small operation. You may also choose to use a heating bulb in your housing area for chicks that are eight days old or younger. This can serve as both a source of heat and a light for your quail chicks. Infrared lights will not disturb the sleep patterns of your quail chicks inside the brooder.

Supplying proper ventilation:

You need to supply a proper amount of fresh air in the brooder. This is very important to allow for gaseous exchange and to keep the respiratory-related infections out of your brooder.

Waterers:

Your quail waterers should be designed in such a way that they will not allow the quail chicks to step into or defecate in them. You should have plenty of drinking water for your quail chicks. Make sure that there is fresh clean water with easy access in a location that will not stress your quail chicks. One of the most common ways that lead to mortality in quail chicks is that they drown in waterers. So, remember to stock them with marbles to help ensure the safety of your quail chicks. The waterers should be cleaned out daily, after about a three-week period remove the marbles.

Tip:

Place your brooder in a location that is away from noise and disturbance to your quail chicks. It needs to be a secure and safe area for your chicks. Raise your quail chicks under healthy and sanitary conditions and you should have no problem running at a profit in your quail farming venture.

Chapter 4. Choosing Your Quail Breed

If you start of your quail farming using a desirable breed then you can expect a desirable output. Depending on what purpose you have behind raising quails, this will largely determine the type of quail breed that you will decide to go with. People will keep distinct types of quail breeds for varied reasons. The reasons differ from keeping them for their eggs, meat or both, or as simple domestic pets.

With the different quail breeds come different personalities. You will need to decide what kind of personality you are seeking in the quails you raise, doing some research can help you to make this decision. Visit local quail farmers and ask them about the personalities of the different breeds, and inquire about the different breeds production capabilities.

As a beginner in quail farming I would suggest starting with a local breed that will be readily available to you. Depending on the type of quail breed you choose will largely determine the kinds of financial gains you will gain from your quail farming.

You are going to have to put some special effort into deciding what the ideal breed of quails will be for you. The steps below offer you some tips and suggestions on ways to help you to make a good decision on the type of flock of quail breed you will choose.

- Research to find out where there are licensed quail farmers in your area. These are people that you should try to contact and ask their advice on the best breed of quail to use in your area. Aim to gain a breed of quails that are best performing breeds from local farmers.

- Visit at least three local quail farmers to see how they each go about raising their quails and observe and learn about the successful methods they use. Remember to ask them about the capabilities of the different breeds.
- Do not purchase a flock of quails that are assorted colors, or are varied sizes or have any kind of deformities. Birds that are varied sizes will fight more, this in turn could result in low unprofitable outputs.
- Stick to one type of quail breed. Do not mix quail breeds as they may end up fighting with each other.
- Find out the mortality rates and history of diseases are with the different quail breeds. Collect this information before you purchase your quails. Most quail breeders will have records of this information in their possession.
- If you are choosing to buy eggs, make sure that they have no abnormalities.

How to tell the difference between the male and female quail:

If you want to raise quails for meat production you will need to know the difference between the two sexes. If you choose to raise quails for egg or meat production you will need to know how to tell the difference between the sexes.

You do not want to discover down the road that you have been raising all male quails with hopes of having eggs laid—you could find yourself waiting a long time for that to happen. Below are some things to watch out for so you can identify if the quail is male or female.

- **The physical appearance:** Once the female quail has matured she will look bigger in size than the male of the same breed and age.
- **Examine quail's vent/cloacae:** This is one of the best ways to distinguish the quail sexes. There are two different ways you can examine the vent. First you can press the area surrounding it with two fingers, if a ball-like lump pops

forward this suggests that the bird is a male. If there is not a ball-like lump then it suggests that the bird is female. Also, if you press the vent and some white foam comes out of it this will also suggest that it is a male. If no foam appears it would suggest that it is a female.

- **Roosting of your quails:** When male quails are around five weeks old several of them will roost (they begin to make soft noise). You can also use the roost to tell the male from the female quail, only the males roost.
- **Check the pattern of the quail's chest:** The female quails have speckled feathers on their chests while the males have plain chest feathers. You will only be able to use this method on quails that have grown enough feathers, about three weeks old or upwards.

Chapter 5. Keeping Your Quails for Commercial Farming

It is well known that within the poultry industry quail farming requires very little investment but can offer you great returns. People wonder if getting into quail farming can really be profitable for them. The truth of the matter is it certainly can be a dream business or it could end up a real nightmare for you, this will depend greatly upon how you approach quail farming.

If you begin with the right breed of quails, with proper housing for them, in a well-suited environment, feed them excellent quality feeds, and supply them with clean drinking water, there is a minimal chance that you will fail at quail farming. However, if you start off with the wrong breed of quail, wrong housing, wrong feeds, and fail to provide them with clean drinking water and a safe and healthy environment then you would be setting yourself up for failure.

One of the best things about raising quails is that you do not need to have a large capital investment to get yourself started into quail farming. The fact that you can make great returns sounds like a win win situation if you follow the correct guidelines in making a successful outcome of your quail farming.

Because of the low capital investment in quail farming and its great returns it is becoming more and more popular by the day. Are aware that is you started your quail farm with just 50 birds, in two or three years you could be taking in millions from your investment? The trick in succeeding well in quail farming is to invest profits of your first year back into your quail farm. After that you can look forward to raking in major profits from your quail farming.

Do some research to discover what you will need to maximize your profits, and take action to make sure that the necessary steps are taken to put your plan into action. You will not go wrong with quail farming if you can focus on production of eggs and chicks. Below I have put together a list of products and by-products of quail farming. You will need to decide what products you are going to focus on producing with your quail farm.

Unfertilized eggs: You can raise female quails that are isolated from males and they will eventually lay unfertilized eggs once they are of egg laying age. When there is no mating between the male and female quails, this results in unfertilized eggs. Producing unfertilized eggs is a common commercial trend with quail farmers. You will be able to find quail eggs being sold at local farmer's markets, and grocery stores. Quail eggs are consumed by many people around the world. They have been scientifically proven to offer many health and medicinal benefits, making them a very popular choice for a meal for many people.

Fertilized eggs: When the male and female quail are together you will produce fertilized eggs. The fertilized eggs have the chance of hatching into quail chicks. To help ensure that the eggs are being fertilized it is best to keep one male with two or three hens.

Quail chicks: Once the incubation period has been successfully completed, the fertilized eggs will hatch into chicks. You will need to be organized and have your customers set up that are interested in acquiring the chicks at a few days old. People who are looking for chicks want to acquire them at a few days old when they are planning to raise them.

Point of lay quail birds: Female quails can begin laying eggs from the age of six weeks onwards. These are the females that are at the egg laying stage. When your chicks hatch, you will need to care for them by providing them with well-balanced feed, medications, fresh water supply, secure and safe environment. Taking these steps is going to help ensure that they will become healthy and productive adult quails for a long period of time.

Manure: Quail waste can be a useful by-product for farming purposes. Quail's droppings are organic in nature and contain high levels of nitrogen. Many crop farmers are looking for it all over the world to spread across their fields.

Meat: You may decide that you are going to raise 'broilers' specifically for meat production, or you may decide to have some layers and some broilers.

When female quails stop laying they are then often slaughtered for their meat. You can pack and freeze quail meat for special order types. The quail meat has a nice taste and it can stay preserved for a long time.

You do not have to purchase already egg-laying female quails

It is difficult to tell the age of a female quail that is already laying eggs. You may want to purchase quails that are just ready to be going into this stage of their development. Or you can choose to raise your quails from chicks.

Quails will begin to gain weight and slow down when they reach full maturity. It has been researched that female quails will lay eggs consistently through the first couple of years of their egg laying stage. In later years, their egg laying may slow down or will stop altogether. Female quails that are four years or more tend to lay eggs that are infertile. The quail farmer could have massive loss if he is not careful, if he is hoping that these birds will give him fertilized eggs for incubation.

If you decide that you want to raise quails for commercial egg production I would suggest that you choose quails that are five weeks or younger. You may choose to hatch your own fertilized eggs, then that would be the best option.

Conclusion

I hope that you and your loved ones will enjoy starting your own quail farm. It will be very easy to setup with low capital investment that could give you great returns! Hopefully the tips and suggestions within these pages will help to make it a bit easier for you getting started as a new quail farmer. The best rule of thumb is to start small and build your way up to be bigger and better! Just think of how great it will be when you will have your own fresh supply of healthy quail eggs! I wish you great success and enjoyment out of your quail farming!

I would like to thank you once again for downloading my book, your support of my work means a great deal to me. I would love to read a review of my book by you on Amazon! Happy quail farming!

FREE Bonus Reminder

If you have not grabbed it yet, please go ahead and download your special bonus report *"DIY Projects. 13 Useful & Easy To Make DIY Projects To Save Money & Improve Your Home!"*

Simply Click the Button Below

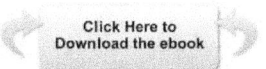

OR **Go to This Page**

http://diyhomecraft.com/free

BONUS #2: More Free & Discounted Books or Products

Do you want to receive more Free/Discounted Books or Products?

We have a mailing list where we send out our new Books or Products when they go free or with a discount on Amazon. Click on the link below to sign up for Free & Discount Book & Product Promotions.

=> Sign Up for Free & Discount Book & Product Promotions <=

OR Go to this URL

http://zbit.ly/1WBb1Ek

www.ingramcontent.com/pod-product-compliance
Lightning Source LLC
Chambersburg PA
CBHW072014280526
45788CB00005B/2043